Arabs and Israelis have been at odds for more than half a century. Here are some key dates in their conflict.

1948-1949: First Arab-Israeli War. Israel won control of western Jerusalem and most of the former Palestine.

1956: Second Arab-Israeli War. The United Nations ended it; neither side gained.

1967: Six Day War. Israel took control of the Gaza Strip, Syria's Golan Heights, Jordan's West Bank, and Egypt's Sinai Peninsula.

1973-1974: Fourth Arab-Israeli War. Israel defeated several Arab nations.

1987-1993: First Palestinian Intifada, or uprising. It ended when talks produced a timetable for creating an independent Palestinian state.

2000-2002: More than 600 people died in the second Palestinian Intifada.

This map shows Israel and several neighboring countries.

Over time, some Arab nations softened their opposition to Israel. In 1979, Israel signed a peace treaty with Egypt, a nation in North Africa. In 1994, Israel signed a peace agreement with the nation of Jordan, Israel's neighbor.

Those treaties didn't end the fighting, because they failed to solve many problems. One of the largest problems involves refugees, people who have fled their country.

During the Arab-Israeli wars, about 850,000 Palestinian Arabs fled their homes. They and their relatives now number about 3.5 million. About 1.2 million of them are living in refugee camps outside Israel. Many Palestinians living outside of Israel wish to return there to build new Palestinian communities.

The Israelis say they can't allow that. About one of every six Israeli citizens is an Arab. But Israelis fear that if the Palestinians living outside its borders moved in, Arab Muslims would soon outnumber Jews. And that, Israelis say, would be the end of their country.

If they can't move into Israel, the Palestinians say, they want their own nation. The group that wants to govern the new state is the Palestinian Liberation Organization (PLO). The PLO already controls the Gaza Strip, an area bordering the Mediterranean. It also controls most of the West Bank, an area of land just west of the Jordan River. In both areas, violent conflict has occurred between Palestinians and Israelis.

The region's Jews and Arabs rarely live together or mix, even in Israel. For the most part, a community in Israel is either Jewish or Arab. The two populations have little to do with one another.

Many Palestinian refugees live in under-developed communities such as this one.

A Divided City

The city of Jerusalem is the capital of Israel. However, many Palestinians who want to establish their own nation hope that Jerusalem will eventually become their capital.

Jerusalem is a holy city for three of the world's largest religions. Jews, Muslims, and Christians all worship at different sites throughout the city. The issue of who will ultimately control the city has caused many conflicts between Muslims and Jews.

One of the most historically important places in Jerusalem is a hilltop area located in the heart of the city. The hilltop is filled with gardens, fountains, and many ancient structures. Because of religious disagreements, though, the area has two different names.

Muslims call the hilltop area Al-Haram al-Sharif, or Noble Sanctuary. A Muslim house of worship called the al-Aqsa Mosque is located there. The mosque is the oldest one in Jerusalem. Also located on the hilltop is the Dome of the Rock. The dome covers a rock that is sacred to the Islamic religion. Muslims believe that Muhammad, the last prophet of Islam, was lifted up to heaven for one night from this rock.

The Dome of the Rock, completed in the year 691, is an Islamic holy site. The dome was originally covered in real gold.

Jews call the hilltop area the Temple Mount. On the western side of the hill is Judaism's most sacred site—the Western Wall. The wall is the last remaining part of an ancient synagogue, or Jewish house of worship. Jews consider the entire Temple Mount area a holy place because of its closeness to the Western Wall.

Every day, Jews from all over the world come to pray at the wall. Worshipers can be found praying at the wall during the day as well as at night. Often, worshipers will write their prayers on a small piece of paper called a *tzetel*. These papers are then inserted into cracks in the wall.

Because of the importance of the Western Wall, Israeli leaders want to ensure that the hilltop area will always be open to Jews. In September 2000, a group of Israeli leaders visited the hilltop. This visit angered many Palestinians who thought the Israelis were planning to take over the area.

After the Israeli leaders left the area, Palestinians organized protests against the Israeli government. The protests quickly turned violent. Both sides began using force, and the violence spread all the way to the Gaza Strip and the West Bank.

Students from an Israeli religious school pray at the Western Wall.

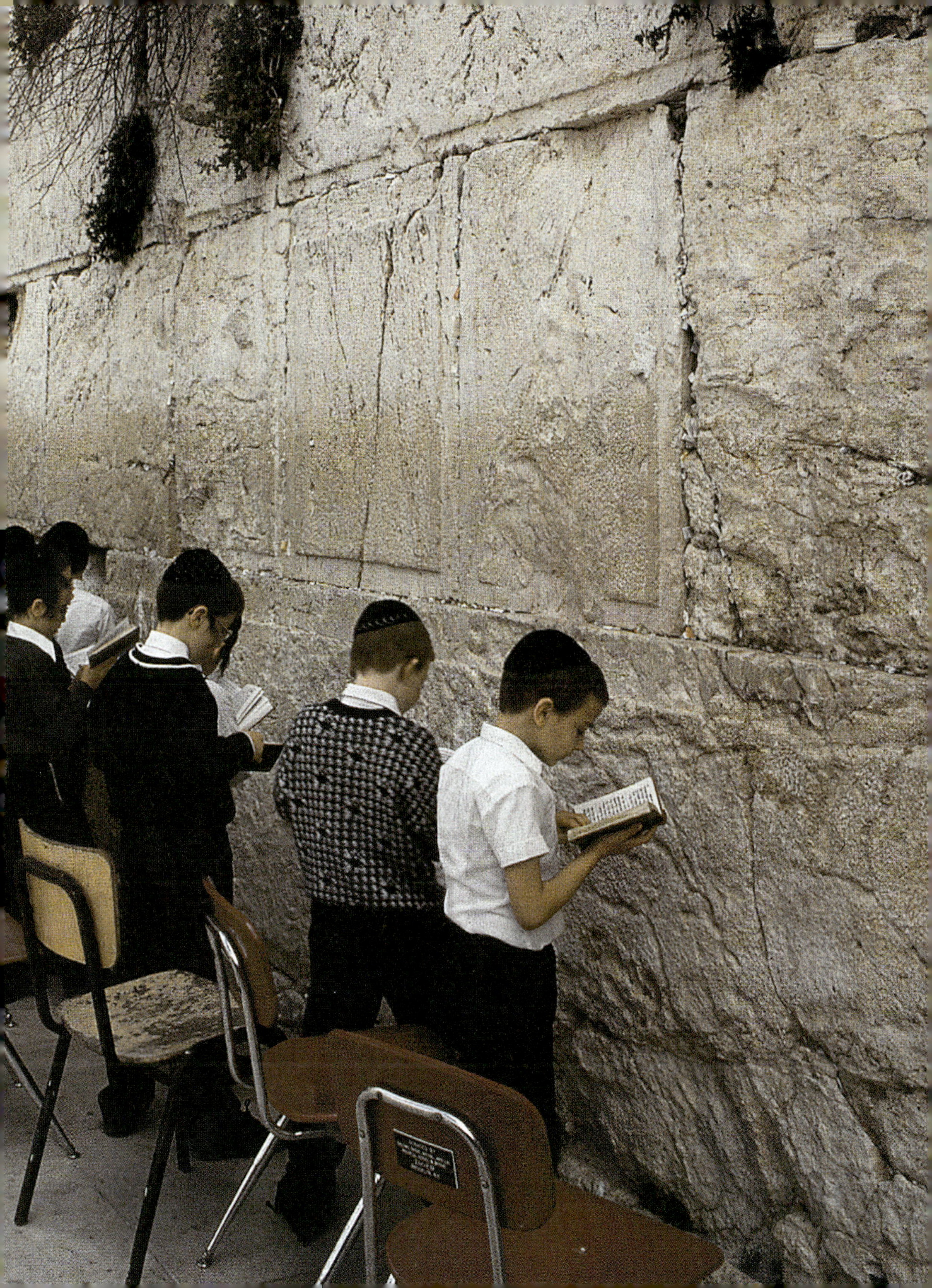

The violence between Israelis and Palestinians that began in October 2000 has continued. More than a thousand people have been killed. The fighting has caused much anger and distrust between the two groups. Many people now question whether Palestinians and Jews in Israel will ever be able to live together.

For the most part, both groups have always lived in separate worlds. Each group has its own language, religion, and way of life. In most of Israel, Jews and Palestinians live in separate neighborhoods and study in separate schools. This is true nearly everywhere except in Neve Shalom/Wahat al-Salam. In this community, Jews and Arabs work, live, and play together. It was Father Hussar's dream to show that these two groups could live in harmony.

The Villagers

Most Arabs and Israelis just want peace. The people of Neve Shalom/Wahat al-Salam want peace, too. And in a small way, they have proven that peace between the two peoples is possible.

Tsipi Zohar (TZIP•ee zoh•HAR) is proud of what the villagers have accomplished. She is a Jewish Israeli who came to the village in December of 1995. Her daughter, Rotem, came with her.

The village, says Zohar, is like no other place in Israel. "Life here so far has completely lived up to our expectations," she says. "I notice . . . the way I relate to language. Though I speak Arabic, it always gave me a strange feeling to hear Arabic spoken in an Israeli city. Now, after living here, Arabic sounds completely familiar."

The community tries to preserve equality by keeping the number of Arab and Jewish residents equal. Another way village leaders try to make things equal is that the Israeli and Palestinian flags are generally not flown. This is done so residents can feel that they are part of a single community. The village's buildings are a mix of Arab and Israeli styles of architecture. On the village's streets both the Hebrew language and the Arabic language can be heard.

Arab and Jewish children play together at the village playground.

The village public schools are places where young people learn to get along. Bright classrooms and patios offer pleasant settings for students to get to know one another.

Teaching Peace

Schooling in Neve Shalom/Wahat al-Salam is special. It is completely bilingual. The teachers speak either Hebrew or Arabic, depending on which language is most natural to them. The students switch back and forth from one language to the other all day. Teaching at every level is built on the idea that the road to peace begins with understanding.

Not all of the 290 children who go to the nursery, kindergarten, and elementary schools come from Neve Shalom/Wahat al-Salam. Nine out of ten of them come from nearby villages.

Arab and Jewish students put on plays and give concerts. They want to show audiences how people with different backgrounds can get along.

15

Class trips and music lessons lead to an appreciation of Jewish and Arab cultures.

The children are taught to appreciate each other's cultures. In part, that means understanding how people think of themselves—as Muslims, for example, or as Jews. It also means accepting others and their traditions, such as holidays. Teachers believe that this openness to others will enable children to understand and accept each other. Parents hope that friendships between Jewish and Arab children will relax the tensions between the two cultures in years to come.

The school system at Neve Shalom/Wahat al-Salam is relatively new. The Education Ministry authorized the kindergarten in 1992. The primary school was given the status of "experimental school" in 1997. Jewish and Arab children sit side by side. They learn together and play together. Neve Shalom/Wahat al-Salam also has another school, the School for Peace. Set up in 1979, it offers many programs for children and adults outside the community.

The School for Peace offers workshops on the conflict between Jewish and Palestinian people in Israel. Some workshops allow Arab and Jewish women to talk about their families and their hopes for the future. Others explore the roots of the conflict that rages outside the village. The school even trains people from other countries.

Older children and adults attend workshops at the School for Peace. It is a place where people can learn to resolve some of their differences.

On the first day of school, students wait to go to their classrooms.

Students' drawings are often labeled in both Hebrew and Arabic.

The Struggle for Equality

Neve Shalom/Wahat al-Salam will never be perfect. Its residents are constantly finding—and in most cases, fixing—problems that arise in the village. For example, some Arab members of the community feel that they should have a stronger voice in community affairs. Others feel that too little time is set aside for the teaching of the Arabic language. School officials hope to overcome these problems in the near future.

Officials also want to develop a better system for dealing with outside tensions. There's no way to escape the fact that violence outside the community affects the way its residents get along. "The crisis outside influences the atmosphere within the village," says Ilan Frisch, who has lived there since 1972.

Ahmad Hijazi is a coordinator at the School for Peace. He organizes meetings to bring Jews and Arabs together. Sometimes he has doubts about whether the village's experiment is working. "It is almost impossible to have equality in a small village when the [world] surrounding [it] is not equal," he says.

Villagers often discuss the conflicts taking place outside Neve Shalom/Wahat al-Salam. The villagers may not always agree with one another, but they do try to respect their neighbors' opinions. They know that many people in Israel look to their community to set a positive example.

Israeli Arab and Jewish women regularly get together to discuss education issues.

Ahmad Hijazi leads a class on improving Arab–Jewish relations.

19

TFK DID YOU KNOW

WHAT DO THE TWO SIDES WANT?

What do the Israelis want? The Israelis want to be able to live in peace in their own country. They want a united Jerusalem.

What do the Palestinians want? The Palestinians want their own nation. They also want Jerusalem as their capital.

What do they both want? Israelis and Palestinians both want control of the Haram al-Sharif/Temple Mount.

Every year the village participates in an international "peace run." Adults and children run together carrying a torch of peace.